Ancient Armenia

Revised

Watercolor by Christine Miller

Anecdotal History of Venture Capital in the USDA Marketing Assistance Project in Armenia and Related Development Experiences

Bill R. Miller

Professor Emeritus of

Agricultural an Applied Economics

University of Georgia

Introduction

After 35 years of teaching and research in higher education, five at Auburn and 30 at the University of Georgia, I retired in June, 1998 as Professor Emeritus of Agricultural and Applied Economics, the University of Georgia. Retirement allowed me to work full-time on my interest in economic development that began after the fall of the Berlin wall in 1989 and continued in 1991-95 with annual appointments in Poland to work on transition of communist Poland to a market economy. Funded by the SEED Act (Support East European Democracy), our work on business planning, with fortuitous backup from the Polish Bank for Agriculture (BGZ), convinced me that venture funding of market infrastructure for agriculture was a key element in developing a market economy and subsequent democratic society

Beginnings: In May, 1998, Tim Grosser, Cooperative State Research, Education and Extension Service of USDA, offered me a position as Project Director and Coordinator of USDA Marketing Assistance Project (MAP) in Armenia. When I saw a project budget that included funds for venture capital and was valued at four million dollars annually, it seemed to be an incredible **opportunity** to actually fund economic recommendations that in my academic career I could only publish as journal articles and hope that someone else would take action. I was more than anxious to give Armenia a try.

Mt. Ararat, Khor Virab Monastery, Grape Vines-- And Noah's Ark? Three photos by Christine Miller with composite overlay work by Leah McPherson

It was in early July of 1998 that Christine and I arrived in Yerevan, the capital of Armenia. Armenia takes pride in being a Christian country (established 301 A.D.) but, beginning in 1921, it became a member of the former Union of Soviet Socialist Republics (USSR). After gaining independence following the 1989 bankruptcy of the communist system, Armenia remained largely committed to their Russian counterparts. If you refer to USDA Marketing Assistance Project—Armenia Memoir (Amazon book, 467 pages) will find more detailed descriptions of Armenia and project data than are presented here. That memoir contains names of the most powerful leaders of the Armenian economy. I listed them in the memoir because I made learning their names an important part of my plans which included avoidance of venture funding for Oligarchs of the former communist regime.

Within a day of arriving in Yerevan I learned that the role of MAP coordinator was far more political and diplomatic than I had realized. Ruth Harris, whom I was replacing, informed me that she had a good relationship with Ambassador Peter Tomsen and she met with him on a weekly basis as a member of his Country Team.

Meeting the Country Team: The Country Team was composed of attaché representing the U.S. Army, U.S. Air Force, USAID, U.S. Treasury, and members of the State Department Foreign Service specialists in Politics, Communications and Personnel. A Foreign Service specialist in Agriculture had never been assigned to Armenia and apparently the Coordinator of MAP, as the highest-ranking member of the U.S. government with funds to spend on agriculture, was appointed to a chair normally reserved for an attaché of the Foreign Agriculture Service (FAS). The appointment was very useful to me as I gained useful feedback on our project. Also, I learned for the first time that all of the funds for MAP were part of the Ambassador's budget for Armenia, at that time more than 100 million dollars. Except for the USAID budget, about 60 million dollars, the MAP budget was one of the largest items in the budget.

One team member had a designation that was never clear. I only knew he had been in Armenia since the beginning of Armenian independence in 1991. Sometime later I asked him what his job was and he said he was in charge of PL 480 sales of U.S. wheat aid to Armenia. It was an important job because in the beginning of Armenian independence from the Soviet Union two of every three loaves of Armenian bread came for American wheat.

PL 480 was a classroom discussion in my teaching at UGA, so I was curious about how he did his job. He said he did it by auction to Armenian mills. When I asked if I could attend an auction he said, "No". He said usually there were only three bidders and they would not like to see me there. I asked my staff why they might not want to see me. The answer was a description of corrupt bidding observed in Armenia: "I bid low this time, you can bid low next time and we will work things out." Did that happen with wheat sales? I don't know, judge it for what it was.

That response was the only information about PL 480 I ever received in Armenia. However, further observations about this member of the country team convinced me he was neither a member of USAID nor of the Department of Agriculture

Meeting the Ambassador: I had been in Armenia less than a week when Ambassador Tomsen requested a meeting in his office. Very noticeable during the meeting was very large photo of a donkey walking up a steep mountain grade and carrying a shoulder fired rocket of the type that so effectively shot down Russian aircraft during the Russian occupation of Afghanistan. There was no U.S. Afghanistan Ambassador during the Russian occupation, but we had Peter Tomsen as a Special Envoy. The picture of the donkey and his rocket seemed to leave little doubt that the U.S. had been involved in the provision of weapons leading to eventual collapse of the Russian occupation, although official U.S. policy persisted that we were not involved in weapons supply.

Ambassador Tomsen wasted no time in casual conversation. His first question was, " What do you plan to do here in Armenia?" I knew exactly what I planned to do. I said MAP has funds to loan and I am going to use them as venture capital to quick-start small firms that accumulate, process, store and distribute food produced from Armenian farms. This plan will provide a market for the thousands of small farms, 4-5 acres, created following the bankruptcy and breakup of State Farms of the former bankrupt and failed USSR. Further, I said, I am not going to loan a single dollar to any Armenian Oligarch or to any member of the former government of Armenia. He said, "Fine, now what are you going to do about the Extension Service? "

This was a more difficult question because, until the beginning of USDA MAP, all of the USDA work in Armenia revolved around their cooperative agreement with the World Bank to create a Federal Extension Service. Under the direction of Ruth Harris, for five years USDA had brought a number of U.S. Extension agents to Armenia. Three U.S. agents were in residence when I arrived and they were carrying out Extension Programs with help from Ministry of Agriculture personnel who were paid from Ruth's budget. Ruth had led the entire effort, including funding and operation of three Marz (regional government) Extension Centers.

When I said I would need some time to investigate our commitments in Armenia, Ambassador Tomsen said, "Well, be careful and don't put another dollar into the Marz Center at Gumrie. I think the government there is totally corrupt." I replied that I would not provide any more funds to any regional Center until I could understand what was happening in the Centers.

Insert: I did investigate the Centers and as a result I discontinued cooperation with the World Bank on the creation of a Federal Extension Service for Armenia. I did fund some mini-grants for Ministry personnel. Ruth Harris, not World Bank, had funded Ministry efforts until I came to Armenia. Very few funds had been expended by World Bank.

Investigation: In my discovery process, I asked one Marz Director: What is your major effort in the new Federal Extension Program? He said, "It was to be producing potatoes for the Army." In the process of discontinuing cooperation with the World Bank, I discovered that the budget for World Bank investment in the Ministry of Agriculture was 17 million dollars. I also discovered that no one had ever explained to Vardan Haikaizian, Armenian counter-part in the USDA agreement with World Bank, of what his new situation would be in the USDA Marketing Assistance Project. Would he continue as the leader of Extension in Armenia?

Haikaizian was aware of the new USDA project and approached me with a proposal that he would privatize the current Armenian Extension effort if MAP would provide more funding. While I would not oppose a privatized Extension effort, I found that World Bank intended to continue with the Armenian Ministry and construct a Federal system without Haikaizian. There was severe Bank criticism of Haikaizian and I could see no future in putting our MAP project in competition with the Armenian Ministry and World Bank; so, I had the unpleasant duty to inform Haikaizian that 80,000 dollars in the unspent budget for his project with USDA would be the end of our association. I did not monitor his spending, but I am sure it went a long way in a country where 10 dollars per month was a common government wage.

Insert: Washington Administrators agreed and sent Ken Farrell (retired former Administrator of USDA Economics Research Service) over to help me communicate with the Armenian Ministry on elements of our new program. My good friend John Ragland (Retired former Director of the USDA Polish/American Extension Project) also participated. John was particularly helpful because he understood my use of venture capital was an extension of small business development we did with help from BGZ bank in Poland for five years (1991-95.

See: Bill R. Miller , H.M. Bahn , M. Drygas , C.H. Rust , 1995, Economics education in a workshop setting: agricultural business plan training in an emerging democracy and market economy.: American Journal of Agricultural Economics, August 1, 1995, Volume: v77 Issue: n3 Page: p462(9) (Poland example)

In my first meeting with the Ambassador he didn't ask anything about education, but I volunteered I hoped to bring U.S. Professors to Armenia on temporary assignments where they would teach courses in market economics in the Armenian Agricultural Academy (AAA). Also, I would like to send some graduate students to study Agricultural Economics in U.S. Universities. Ambassador Tomsen seemed satisfied with my answers and that was the end of the meeting.

My weekly meetings with his Country Team continued and provided me with updates on current events in the country. The meetings were interesting as I was able to gain insight into the Armenian economy. I also joined the security apparatus of the Embassy and received my security nickname of "Bulldog", but pronounced by Armenian security guards as "Bawl dawk".

Dinner with the Ambassador; Several weeks after our first meeting I received a note from the Ambassador. He was hosting a dinner for Minister of Agriculture Vladimir Movsesyan. It was to be a very private dinner, including only the Ambassador, the Minister, me and our wives.

At the dinner the Ambassador and the Minister professed to be great friends, and I think they were. Ambassador asked me repeat some of what we had discussed in his office. I did so and included my comments on doing work in the area of economics education. Minister Movsesyan who, at that time had administrative control of the Academy, provided some positive comments and I thought the Ambassador was pleased with my remarks.

In the parking lot after dinner I discovered how pleased he was. In a very casual manner, Ambassador Tomsen said, "I thought Movsesyan was very receptive of your comments and will support American Professors who could come and teach economics at the Academy; so, at the next budget hearing add another million dollars to your budget."

Later, after reflection, I believed that the real purpose of the dinner was for me to communicate my plans to the Minister so Ambassador Tomsen could observe his reaction.

Insert; At the time of meetings with Ambassador Tomsen I had knowledge of a USDA contract in the area of higher education. Early in the Armenia work, USDA, under guidance of Ruth Harris, had started a contract with Fresno State University. USDA provided me with a briefing on the program prior to my going to Armenia. After the briefing I traveled to Fresno, California and consulted with the Dean in charge of the contract. He made a particular point that Fresno State Professors would only be able to visit Armenia during the summers. They were on nine-month contracts and were available only in the summer.

Six Fresno Professors had been coming each summer as a group and referred to themselves as the California Six-Pack. They usually stayed about a month and wrote reports on how to improve the curriculum of the Armenian Agricultural Academy (AAA). Reports of the Six-Pack were not well received by the faculty of AAA. When I asked AAA Rector Terverdian what he thought about the Fresno program, he said, "I would rather have their air-fare and expense account; with that I could run AAA for a year." Also, there was no teaching by the Fresno Professors. Unfortunately for the Fresno contract, the Armenian Agricultural Academy offered no courses in the summer. Summer work by Fresno Professors did not seem to be a good fit for my plan of teaching agribusiness courses in English.

During the time I was reviewing the Fresno contract, the Fresno Coordinator was in Yerevan and he became involved in controversy with an Embassy guard. I was told the incident attracted some displeasure from Ambassador Tomsen. Hearing of the incident, and given my new-found relations with Rector Terverdian, I wasted no time sending a letter to Fresno State saying their services were no longer needed; their annual contract for 500,000 dollars was now null and void. I sent a copy of my letter to Ambassador Tomsen. He sent it back with his initials and one comment—OK. I greatly admired his comment and started using it myself on a number of mini-grant projects we funded with Academy faculty. My favorite use can still be found inscribed in concrete on a mountain stream dam we built to carry water two miles to an Armenian village. It says, BRM, OK.

I had plans to continue development of education with Rector Terverdian of the Armenian Agricultural Academy and I wanted to solidify our commitment with Ambassador Tomsen. I sent him the following memo.

August 17, 1998

Dear Ambassador Tomsen,

I would like to meet with you for about 30 minutes to discuss the USDA MAP budget for 1999, and to talk more about the scholarship program mentioned during our dinner meeting with Minister Movsesyan.   .

Bill R. Miller Project Director and Coordinator of USDA MAP

Ambassador Tomsen encouraged me to continue with the Academy and so, on August 28, I concluded the following agreement with Rector Terverdian (AAA). The following memo is in the files of MAP.

Memorandum of Understanding

Between

USDA Marketing Assistance Project

And

Armenian Agricultural Academy

USDA Marketing Assistance Project (MAP) agrees to renovate the fourth-floor space directly above the existing third floor space in the Armenian Agricultural Academy (AAA). The renovated space will be known as the Agribusiness Teaching Center (ATC). The Center will contain two classrooms, a learning center, office spaces for three instructors, and a restroom. These spaces will be fully equipped to supply the needs of teaching the new Agribusiness Curriculum and will be ready to begin operations on September 1, 2000.

USDA MAP agrees to expenditures of no more than 110,000 dollars for total renovation and equipment needs. The Education Manager of USDA MAP will specify equipment needs. USDA MAP building committee will determine the design of the space. USDA MAP agrees to supply AAA with receipts for all payments made for goods and services required to complete the project.

AAA agrees to accept funds from the donor community and deposit them in a fund known as the Armenian/American Development fund for AAA. The Rector will fund applied research grants and extension mini-grants from donations to this fund, up to the limit provided by USDA MAP grants to the fund. Decisions on these grants will be made by the Project Coordinator of USDA MAP in keeping with priorities determined for a national program of applied research and extension. The Rector and the Project Coordinator will make a mutual determination of members appointed to an Advisory Committee that will determine national priorities.

Bill R. Miller, MAP COORDINATOR   Submitted August 28, 1998

Creating the Agribusiness Teaching Center: With the funds from Ambassador Tomsen, and with the agreement of Rector Terverdian (AAA) secured, I began the process of building space for the Agribusiness Teaching Center (ATC). I hired the former chief architect for the city of Yerevan and we set about drawing plans for renovating space that had been under construction at AAA. When I asked Rector Terverdian what he thought about adding a floor to his building, he said, "Go as high as you want."

We did a competitive bid process and the contract was won by Kilikia Construction Company. They did what I thought was an excellent job by providing a space equal to what I enjoyed at the University of Georgia. I feel compelled to offer a few anecdotes about uniqueness of the construction. One: I have witnessed the finishing process of dry-wall construction, but I have never witnessed a process of finishing the final surface with a six-foot 2x4. The result was great. Two: I had to hire a member of the Ambassador's staff, an American consultant hired for work on the Embassy, to show Kilikia how to install back-vented pipe for the sewer system of toilets we included in the new home for Agribusiness Teaching Center. Back-vented plumbing that prevents "sewer gas" from entering the building was apparently unknown to Kilika. The building was completed by spring of 1999 and we had a formal opening ceremony, during which I presented a framed letter to Rector Terverdian

My letter said, **"The USDA Marketing Assistance Project, acting on behalf of the U.S. Embassy Mission to Armenia, dedicates this building renovation for the development of teaching, research and extension in Armenia and presents it to the Armenian Agricultural Academy.**

We had a ribbon cutting ceremony attended by the new U.S. Ambassador Michael Lemmon and his wife Michele, John Nichols of Texas A&M University and Dan Dunn.

Ribbon Cutting at the Grand Opening of ATC

Bill Miller, Ambassador Lemmon, Dan Dunn, Rector Terverdian, and Michelle Lemmon at the opening of the Agribusiness Teaching Center----John Nichols is in the background behind Dan Dunn.

I had named Texas A&M to be the leader of efforts to bring U.S. Professors to the Agribusiness Teaching Center (ATC) and John Nichols hired Dan Dunn to be one of the first to teach an agribusiness class in English. Dan Dunn and Emerson Babb, University of Florida, began the teaching program and Dan remained as teacher and Director of ATC operations for many years.

Moving ahead to Graduation 2006: I returned to speak to the graduating class of ATC; they were now part of a new Armenian National Agrarian University (ANAU). My speech in English did not need translation for the graduating class. They were all fluent in English; It was a requirement to enter the program.

Graduation 2006 at Agribusiness Teaching Center

Bill Miller, Rector Terverdian, Minister of Education, Translator, and U.S. Ambassador John Evans (L,R)

I made an address to the graduates during which I described the importance of the wheel in economic development, and I closed with the thought of how a linchpin was needed to keep the wheel working. So, I challenged the agribusiness graduates to be the linchpin that would keep the Armenian economy on course to be a successful market economy.   A friend who watched the speech said, "-- I don't believe they got it".   I think they did. I have hope.

Rector Terverdian presented me a Gold Medal Award and introduced his award ceremony with the following speech.

"--many USDA TDY consultants helped this Biblical country create its prosperous future. As an Armenian, I pay the biggest tribute to these great Americans. I would like to state the following: about them. " -- "The economic role of these people at the dawn of the 21st century is no less critical for Armenia than the political role that their great countryman Henry Morgenthau (the US Ambassador to Ottoman Empire,

1913- 1916) played in the beginning of the 20th century and still plays for the rest of Armenian history. --ATC and ICARE foundations are happy to host one of these great Americans, Bill Miller

The University also honored my return with this press release:

Bill Miller, Professor Emeritus, University of Georgia and Honorable Professor of the Armenian National Agrarian University, visited Armenia to participate in the ATC graduation ceremony on June 4. It was Dr. Miller's first visit since he left Armenia upon completion of his direction of the USDA Marketing Assistance Project in Armenia in 1998-2000. During his work, the entire Armenian agribusiness sector was rehabilitated and adapted to the new market economy. It experienced unprecedented modern development through USDA MAP's financial, technical, and marketing efforts. Under Dr. Miller's leadership, dozens of old and newly emerged fruit and vegetable processing enterprises, wineries, and dairy processing factories restarted or started successful production, marketing, and export activities due to the use of American taxpayer funding.

At the ATC graduation ceremony, the Rector of the Armenian National Agrarian University, Arshaluys Terverdyan, and Bill Miller met as old friends. Rector Terverdyan had prepared a pleasant surprise for the U.S. Ambassador to Armenia, John Evans and to Bill Miller: they were awarded the Armenian National Agrarian University's Gold Medal for their significant input in the development of agrarian education and research in Armenia.

The graduates of ATC have compiled a remarkable record. The original concept of offering graduate assistantships on a competitive basis for further study in the US was continued by MAP. After the first six assistantships were awarded in 1999, the scope of the offers was limited to two assistantships per year. Seven of the first 12 awarded returned for work in Armenia.

Some Students of Agribusiness Teaching Center

According to the ATC Career Placement and counseling Center (CPCC) in 2006, about 74% of ATC graduates were currently employed. Most of those not currently employed were working on advanced degrees, or serving in the military. All are fluent in English.

In addition to working in Armenia and Republic of Georgia, some ATC graduates worked in the U.S., Canada, Hungary, Paraguay, Russia, Germany, The Netherlands, Belgium, Malawi and Afghanistan. ATC graduates had pursued, or had completed, MS or PhD degrees in the universities of: Armenia (3), Republic of Georgia (3), United States (9), and Europe (5).

In 2006, I asked Rector Terverdian to comment on the growth of his Academy into Armenian National Agrarian University, ANAU, as a significant University. He said that ATC had become such drawing card for students that he could not admit all of them to ATC. During several years of offering ATC in English his enrollment increased from four thousand students to nine thousand and he began a new University curriculum in agri-business outside of ATC.

Teaching agribusiness and teaching English continues in 2019 as a major part of the Armenian National Agrarian University (ANAU) and you can now earn a Master of Agribusiness degree for academic study in the Agribusiness Teaching Center. The degree has been recognized by the Higher Education Commission of the European Union.

The Venture Investment Project: In addition to development work on ATC, I continued to advise Ambassador Tomsen on our program of venture capital to be used in developing a marketing system for farm production.

September 4, 1998

To: Brady Kiesling   Copy to Ambassador

From: Bill R. Miller Coordinator and Director of USDA MAP

Subject: USDA Program of Work

MAP Results to September, 1998:

** After the end of the Armenian/American Extension Project, the activities of USDA continued in Armenia as a Marketing Assistance Project.

USDA supplies marketing expertise and strategic loans to stimulate the demand for farm production. Loans are targeted to eliminate bottlenecks in the marketing system. A simple example is provision of glass jars from Bulgaria to keep canning plants open. Loans have also been made to put entire processing plants back into operation. Because of capital rationing in Armenia, many processing plants would remain closed without USDA assistance; thousands of farmers would have no market outlet.   Examples to see include:

    Meghri Cannery for berries, fruit and walnuts

    VAN 777 a small winery operated by Mihran Manasirian

    Tavoush Cannery for berries and fruit

    Armavir Tomato Cannery

    Amassia Cheese Plant

    Ashotck Swiss Cheese

Export of Tomato and Peppers, production of seed, by Volovia Ghazarian

The total value of all USDA loans is 1.4 million dollars 1n 1997-98. A portfolio of 2 million is expected by early 1999.

** USDA is also assisting a joint venture investment between Armenians and Americans that could process approximately 50 percent of Armenian production of fruit for juice. Confidential files of Ambassador Peter Tomsen contain details of progress to date.

** USDA has an academic enrichment program for the Armenian Agricultural Academy and seeks to integrate currently separated functions of teaching, research and technology transfer. An integrated program is needed for an efficient program of marketing assistance for an efficient science that will produce a market revolution in Armenia. Rector Arshalouys Terverdyan leads this effort with USDA support.

** USDA consults with the Ministry of Agriculture on all of its work in Armenia. Program planning takes place with Minister Vladimir Movsesyan.

Program leaders at USDA MAP include

    Bill R. Miller, Project Coordinator   Ph. 40 79 51 (Cell)

    Ruth Harris, Extension Manager

As you can see from the September memo I had retained Ruth Harris, former Project Coordinator of MAP as a part of our staff. In questioning our staff about past events in MAP I found that she had promised to bring a lawsuit against USDA if she was removed from her job. Her complaint included a claim of unlawful use of project funds by a USDA Administrator on temporary assignment in Armenia. Sorry, although certainly interesting in a soap-opry manner of speaking, I will not repeat the details.

I found Ruth to be very helpful with project history and a very capable associate. I was not going put my scarce time into any round of " She said He did." lawsuit. My view was that USDA had hired her and if they wanted her removed it was their problem, not mine. Before she was given a new job in the U.S. she was successful in holding, in Yerevan, a United Nations Conference on the "Women in Development". Women from all over the world descended on Yerevan for a week to talk about women as leaders. Her principal cooperator, and leader among women in Yerevan, was the wife of a leading Oligarch. Yes, I was impressed.

Use of Venture Capital: Our clientele for venture capital expanded rapidly from the 97-98 base. In the next two years one of the fastest growing areas was the dairy sector. Milk and milk products are staples of Armenian diet, but farm production was down and quality was non-existent. One of our staff, Felix Vardanian, suggested that if we could cool the milk at farm level then more milk could reach consumers. He was right; and to me it sounded like a great way to use venture capital to improve the market for farm production. I asked Felix to contact Alfa Laval, a distributor of milk handling equipment (Tumba, Sweden). He did and found they could easily provide 500-liter milk cooling tanks. We ordered one; Felix and I delivered it.

Leasing. The milk cooling project also gave MAP a new method of financing development---- leasing venture capital. My first look at our books in the summer of 1998 showed that a little more than 30 percent of the loans from 96-97 were non-performing.   Our repayment record was so bad that HSBC bank, holder of our capital funds, called me in to their office and said they would prefer that we move our funds to another bank. Our clientele were giving their bank a bad name.

We did move the funds and I decided we needed a new method of providing funds to risky investments. I committed a million-dollar fund as the basis for a leasing company. We ran the company out of our office; **Samvel Mkhitryan agreed to manage the project for 6 percent of lease collections** and it became the first leasing company in Armenia.

A group of international consultants showed unexpectedly in my office and said that my leasing company was a bad idea. I never found out how they made their way to my office. P.S. It was not a bad idea as we eventually leased more than a million dollars of equipment with no losses. Other leasing companies now operate in Armenia; when I returned to Armenia in 2006 our initial company had been privatized and was still providing leases.

_{Letter from manager of the first leasing company in Armenia and who was first employed by MAP in 1998.}

August, 2005 from Samvel Mkhitryan

Dear Dr. Miller,

    Several times I started a letter to you, but it's still uncompleted. I remember how the leasing company was started, our first lease and first leaser. The name of the head of milk collection center is Sasun Markaryan and he is doing a great job. At this moment, his collection center has paid back three lease agreements, and they are the owner of the two milk cooling tanks, milking machines and a milk truck. The Lejan milk association is the first and one of the best companies.

    Now the leasing company is working with more than 75 local companies, and lease agreements are worth from $1,600 up to $200,000. Our clients are: Artashat Cannery, Meghry Cannery, MAP, Ashtarak Kat, Marianna (the last two are dairy producers), Tamara Fruit, more the 10 cheese making companies, etc.

In August 2003, our leasing company was re-registered in Central Bank of RA as a leasing, credit company with the special license of operating under CB regulations. During the last four years, the leasing company has brought to Armenia agricultural machinery, food processing equipment and complete production lines for canneries and winemakers for the total price of 1,700,000 USD.

Water color by Christine Miller

The First Leasing Contract: MAP leased the first cooling tank to Lejan village. There were no up-front costs and the village could make payments from milk sales. When we delivered the tank, I advised Mayor Sasun that if he couldn't make payments we would move the tank to another village. Their tank, nor any tank from future leases in many villages, was ever moved. Their 500-liter tank was so successful we had to order a larger tank of 1,000 liters. You can see more in my longer memoir (Amazon Memoir).

The cooling tank was the first of a success that resulted, in my last count, of 35 dairy processors who developed milk collection and distribution along with production of new cheese products and other milk products. One of the new firms produced the first pasteurized milk in Armenia. Our outreach in providing venture capital continued in other areas and included most of the fruit, vegetable and animal products of Armenia. Again, I refer you to my memoir (Amazon) for a complete description of 65 farm marketing firms that were either started or assisted in start-up by MAP.

Can Venture Capital Fail? Providing venture capital for agribusiness development was a driving force in MAP, but simply providing money for risky ventures requires more than just providing funds, buying equipment and constructing buildings. Notable failures by the U.S. Army can be citied when the human dimension of building market infrastructure was not a principle concern. This was a fatal mistake; local ownership and management must be a primary concern.

Good examples of failed management and ownership can be found in a book by Peter Van Buren, "We Meant Well: How We Helped Lose the Battle for Hearts and Minds of the Iraqi People". He wrote many reports concerning millions of dollars spent during his work with the Army's Provincial Reconstruction Teams (PRT). I cite only two of his most egregious testimonials of using risk capital in ventures that did not include local management initiative.

*Van Buren, " We built a milk collection center that had no way of getting milk to market, or farmers willing to produce milk."

*Van Buren, " We built a chicken processing plant, at a cost of three million dollars, that had no market and had no chickens to process. At times one could buy 50 to 100 chickens in a local market to demonstrate use of the plant." In other testimonials Van Buren reported that while there were bundles of cash lying around, they had no appropriate expertise in how to use venture capital.

Testimonials from Armenian Users of MAP Venture Capital:

The most detailed testimonial of MAP success was given by Samvel Avetysian, a member of the Armenian Parliament. The source of his data about MAP came from interviews he did with MAP staff. I don't present them as official data, but I can verify they are accurate for the time when he collected his information.

Samvel Avetysian said the following about MAP:

"More than 2,500 permanent jobs were created in agribusiness. The number of farmers benefited from the MAP projects is more than 40,000. Strategic, micro-enterprise, production credit loans and grants have been provided for market assistance. The Armenian Agricultural Academy is the principal recipient of grants for work with farmers and students and for creation of human capital. MAP accomplishments include: intensive efforts in market promotions in the Russian market; export of dozens of tons of cheeses, hundreds of thousands of bottles and jars of wine, fruit preserves and juices; creation of dairy, seed potato, tomato growers' associations; goat breeding program; variety trials; technology assessment of Extension programs jointly with the World Bank Ag Reform Project; construction and reconstruction of 8 deep water wells for irrigation and drinking available for 38,000 villagers; 30 production credit clubs; Agribusiness Teaching Center at AAA; establishment of AgroLeasing LLC (which has provided over $1,000,000 leased agricultural equipment for MAP-supported agribusinesses), Foundation for Applied Research and Agribusiness, Small farm Water Management Research Center, and 86 extension youth clubs with more than 1,000 members, and others."

Thanks to Samvel for his efforts to document the success of MAP. I would emphasize again that to be successful with providing venture capital for agricultural marketing there must be a search for those individuals who understand local farm production and who know the location and needs of local consumers. Under those conditions, venture capital can become part of continuing ambition and willingness of local people to work toward personal goals. My outstanding Armenian staff looked for those managers and they found them. A staff of 50 members played a key role in the success of MAP.

Important results of MAP are found in testimonials from the people assisted by MAP staff. Some come from the book: "The USDA 12-year story of partnership with Armenia". Other stories I cite include a testimonial from Marian Alexandrian (of my staff) concerning her work with credit clubs and I include a testimonial from Mayor Sasun of Lejan village.

Owner Aghasi Baghdasaryan of Genatum Winery said:

"I always dreamed of starting my own business in wine-making , but I was always faced with financial challenges that I could not solve on my own. MAP made it possible."

Manager Martirossyan of Golden Goat Cheese Mfg. said:

"USDA was the only organization that was willing to run the risk and provide financial support to get us going. USDA invested in remote villages where nobody else would go, and in the process created nearly 700 jobs, farm production and marketing, that are connected just with our business."

Manager Assadour Haroutunian of Duster Melanya Cheese Plant said:

"Back in the beginning of our factory, it was just unimaginable that an organization like the USDA would come to you and offer suggestions to improve the quality of your product and expand your business. It shocked us to the point that we actually worried about taking out even a small loan from USDA MAP to start growing our business.

Hyich Ghooilyan of Vahan Mountain Village said:

"Our people get cash money for the milk they bring to our milk cooling center each day, so that means our villages can now buy books, clothes and food for their children."

Mariana Alexandrian, our Credit Club Manager, gave her view of 500,000 dollars of personal equity saved by MAP Credit Club members in just over 50 micro-credit clubs who were provided venture capital. Said Mariana, "The MAP Credit Club program is not just about money, it is about changing lives."

Insert: A detailed description of these unique credit clubs can be found in Armenia Memoir (See Amazon). Basically, MAP provided a loan of venture capital to farmers on which a credit club member paid interest on his loan, but not to USDA; he paid it to ownership of equity by his club. MAP only received payment of principal which was placed in a revolving fund for future loans. I planned about one million dollars for the revolving fund. More than 1.5 million dollars were eventually used by MAP to support farmers who were delivering products to our start-up marketing firms. The clubs created over 500,000 dollars of personal equity.

Comments about a cooling tank and credit clubs from Mayor Sasun of Lejan Village:

Sasun said, "After a period of time we established a cooperative starting with only one cooling tank. There were 37 farmers from our village bringing milk when we sent the first tank of milk to Yerevan. Soon farmers from five other communities joined the cooperative. There were 180 farmers in the five villages.

Daily we were collecting about 400 liters of milk (about .4 ton). Now, in 2006, we have as much as 3.5 tons of milk daily. Due to the cooperative we began to increase the use of arable land and we purchased a vacuum tank and truck to bring milk in from the mountains. Now, every morning we are sending milk to the cheese processing plant at Tashir and milk continues to come in from surrounding communities. Another shipment is made daily to Vanidzor. If there is ever a surplus we deliver to Ashtorok.

With the help of MAP, we established a credit club to increase production. This provided a very big push in the whole community when we established the credit club. First, we used the credit club to purchase more cows. In 2001 there were about 500 cows in the villages. Currently, in June of 2006, there are about 1,100 cows. Now, with more cash from milk, we can afford to buy corn that increases our milk production.

We remember that in the beginning we bought milk from families who had no cash to buy bread or flour. Now you won't find these kinds of families and we are very grateful to you. I don't see how we could have been in this state without MAP.

The credit club loans started the whole chain of production. I would like to present some numbers on credit clubs. We have a club in each of four villages in our cooperative and in the beginning they had a total of 80 members. The total amount of their first loans was $48,800 and all of it was USDA money. In 2006 there were 109 members in the clubs and they borrowed $145,000 of which the USDA part was $87,000 and the club's own money (equity from our own interest payment) was $58,000. In the beginning farmers could use about $600 each. Now they average borrowing about $1,300 per year and with new production they can pay it back.

We are about 40 percent self-owned.

The MAP credit club model was a unique approach to microfinance and was the starting point for new agricultural credit legislation in Armenia. Using MAP funds, I sent six Armenian legislators to the United States to study U.S. legislation for farm credit. On their return to Armenia they were assisted by U.S. finance specialists, Harshbarger and Womack, in drafting new agricultural credit law for Armenia. Their work now supports a new agricultural cooperative bank in Armenia. This is their report.

Farmers Take Charge of Credit

by Ed Harshbarger and Jasper Womack,

USDA Farm Credit Administration

and U. S. Congressional Research Service

"Give them credit, Armenian farmers know a good deal when they see it. In this case, however, it goes beyond observing; they are taking matters into their own hands by forming credit clubs for their mutual benefit, with a little monetary help from USDA to help them get started. This practice is a wonderful example of farmers joining together to establish a cooperative organization to promote their mutual interests and financial welfare.

During our 3-week tour in November to help parliament draft credit legislation, we had an opportunity to visit 6 of the 23 clubs that have been established by USDA in the last three years. It was rewarding to learn that most of them are succeeding, even with all the weather problems of the past year. We were impressed with the clubs' leadership and the determination of the membership to repay their loans and make their organizations profitable. For many producers, these small loans are their only source of credit because banks won't lend to them at all. Or if they do, the terms are unaffordable.

The production credit club program is a model of self-help. The membership is generally limited to a small number of people with a common enterprise, e.g., wheat or dairy production. The members cross-guarantee each other's loans from the club, which ensures repayment discipline and effective controls. Although the borrower receives 85% of the loan proceeds at origination and repays 100% when it matures, the "interest" actually goes into two separate accounts in the borrower's name at a bank. Thus, the loan is interest free. If the member remains in good standing, the accounts can become a source of savings for both the farmer and the club. This new money can then be used to make additional loans and help the organization grow.

We all appreciate the immense challenges faced by Armenia's farmers. The credit clubs are but one example of how they are working together to make something good happen, one small step at a time."

The success of the Credit Clubs continued past the end of the MAP project in 2005. The Armenian NGO CARD sent me the following letter in 2008.

July 7, 2008
Dear Dr. Miller,

I would like to update where we are today. Last week CARD registered new AgroCredit lending organization at the Central Bank.
So, starting next week we can offer leasing and credit to CARD (former USDA MAP) clients and strengthen our sustainability. We invested 1,5 million USD and will invest another 1,5 million next year.
We are also thinking how we can work with the best credit clubs and how we can develop this concept based on business approach. So, we are going to have MAP model based on business approach.

Kind regards,
Gagik

Credit Clubs were frequently managed by wives

The testimonials for use of credit and cooling tanks are evidence of venture capital success, but, for me, the most poignant of all testimonials was my conversation with a woman who brought a quart of milk to a milk cooling center. She said she couldn't bring any more, because "---her cow was her main source of food."

To be sure, the translation to English of these comments does not exactly match the Armenian words, but I observed all of these projects and the sincerity of the participants was not in doubt.

Dairy Goats: Building on our success with dairy cows we continued development of milk and cheese with dairy goats. I have a treasured memento from the Golden Goat Cheese Company. Before I left Armenia, they gave me a Golden Goat Award. It was a gold painted plaster goat, but I treasured it nevertheless. The expansion of goat cheese output had been a result of ARID Breeding Center work that almost doubled productivity of goat milk in Armenia.

The ARID Center (Armenia Dairy Goat Breeding Center) still operates in Armenia and was inspired by the work of Gagik Sardarian who pointed out to me that one of the highest value food products in Armenia was produced by some of the lowest paid farmers. A typical goat herd is located in a village where a villager may own one or more goats; goats leave the village in the morning as one herd and return for milking in the evening.

I arranged to purchase breeder goats in America and coordinated the project with Deputy Minister Khachatryan.

April 3, 2000

First Deputy Minister Armen Khachatryan

Ministry of Agriculture Armenia

Dear First Deputy Khachatryan,

I have agreed with the President of American Dairy Goat Association to purchase registered dairy goats in the U.S. and I have the cooperation of the U.S. Department of Agriculture Veterinarians who will certify the goats for export.

Recommend shipment is 6 Toggenburg does, 3 Toggenburg bucks, 6 Alpine does, 3 Alpine bucks, 4 Saanen does, 2 Saanen bucks, 4 Nubian does and 2 Nubian bucks. This would total 20 does and 10 bucks.

Each animal will be registered in the American Dairy Goat Association (ADGA) and will have an individual registration certificate showing the information on the animal along with the information on the parents and grandparents. All animals will be selected by the President of ATGA for milking ability, soundness of health and breed character

The shipment can be made on April 29 via a World Food Flight. In order to ship on April 29, you will need to request the information on the attached page that will allow the USDA Inspector to allocate time to certify health of the animals. I need you to return the attached page no later than April 6 to allow shipment on the 29th. If shipment is not made on the 29th, I do not at this time have an alternative shipment date. The attached letter is parallel to the letter that I used to requested goat semen.

Best regards and thank you for your leadership in this project.

Bill R. Miller, Project Coordinator, USDA MAP

ARID Center was founded around MAP imports of male and female goats of Alpine, Nubian, Toggenburg and Saneen breeds. P.S. They were the only animals ever transported by a World Food Flight, they built special cages for the trip.

Ambassador Michael Lemmon and I made comments at the opening of the Center in ARID Center in 2000. Ambassador Lemmon announced that he would also sign a long term approval of sharing genetic materials between the U.S. and Armenia. -----Personal note: A Toggenburg female goat adopted Christine, following her around and nibbling at her fingers like a puppy whenever we visited the herd.

Status in 2006: In 2006 the industry exported approximately 35 tons of goat cheese valued at more than $300,000, and utilized milk cooling tanks at six cheese processors and at six milk collection centers. About 300 farmers were delivering milk to the cooling tanks and farm production was supported by three Credit Clubs. U.S. TDY cheese specialists have supported development of the market by introducing seven new kinds of cheese that were added to the Armenian specialty of "buried goat cheese." Exports to the U.S. and Russia are common.

Gagik Sardaryan, Head of CARD, Narine Babyan, Head of ARID Breeding Center, and the Manager of a Goat Cheese plant in an Armenian Village with a typical milk cooling tank.

Some Final Results of Venture Capital: By the end of MAP in 2005 the project had provided venture capital and/or technological advice to 65 nascent firms that supported expanded farm output. A United Nations study forecast that Armenia would soon be placed in the category of countries that had food security. In 2002, after continuing all of the projects started in 98-2000, USDA named the MAP project as the, "Best International Project of the Year." Throughout its life the MAP project expended 80 million dollars and used over 300 American specialists on short term assignments, and who supplemented the work of 50 Armenian specialists on the MAP staff.

Although most of the MAP funds were devoted to venture capital investment and agribusiness education in what is now the Armenian National Agrarian University, we had other projects that contributed to Armenian food security.

Our Credit Clubs for more than 700 farmers provided the clientele for a cooperative agricultural bank. The six members of the Armenian Parliament we sent to the U.S studied farm credit and on their return wrote new legislation establishing coops in agricultural credit. When they submitted their legislation, there were, for the first time in Parliament history, no dissenting votes for approval. An Agricultural Cooperative Bank now operates in Armenia.

Vegetable planters

New vegetable varieties were introduced; we developed youth clubs throughout the nation based on the U.S. 4-H model. By air freight we brought 11,500 day-old chicks to produce hatching eggs of new breeds of chickens (Arbor Acres) for both eggs and broilers. Also, MAP distributed 6,000 Tetra-H laying hens for production of hatching eggs. Much of this work was accomplished via mini-grants to faculty, in what is now ANAU, who coordinated their work with MAP staff.

We established a National Speaking Contest for youth based on the model for 4-H clubs. My favorite speech was from a young student, no more than age 15, who said the brother of the Armenian Prime Minister needed to clean up environmental pollution being created by his concrete mixing plant. Unfortunately, I never learned the result of his speech.

The MAP youth program was widespread in Armenia and was always noticed by visitors from the U.S. Pamela Karg wrote the following about Armenian 4-H. (From the USDA Haiystan newsletter of October, 2004.) -- "Whether crossing state lines or country borders, 4-H is there". -- "That was a discovery by Sauk County's Pamela Karg. She traveled to Armenia to assist a humanitarian program – the United Methodist Committee on Relief (UMCOR) – with public relations projects. During the trip, she attended several harvest festivals and discovered 4-H everywhere."

Results from Village Wells: In late 1998, Mike Sigler, U.S. Defense Department Attaché who served with me on the Country Team , told me that European Command, EUCOM, would accept humanitarian grant proposals for digging village wells. I submitted a request for 250,000 dollars that was granted and work began in late 2000. Work continued after I left Armenia and eventually resulted in total funding of 1.1 million dollars for 74 village wells benefitting more than 170,000 village residents.

At the same time, I submitted the grant proposal to EUCOM, I submitted a proposal to the new Minister of Agriculture, Zavin Gevorgian, for a **Small Farms Water Management Extension Center** to be located in AAA. The Center would be initially funded by MAP and would be headed by Dr. Gurgen Yeghiazaryan. The concept was approved and was initially funded by MAP in 2000. During my visit in 2006 the Center was still in operation, but now funded by the Ministry of

Education, and Dr. Yeghiazaryan was the Center Head in what is now the Armenian National Agrarian University.

I nominated Dr. Yeghiazaryan as manager of the Center because of outstanding work he did for MAP on development of gated pipe irrigation systems.

Gated Pipe Irrigation

But developing the Rind village water supply was probably Dr. Gurgen Yeghiazaryan's most unique water project. Rind village is located in Vyots Dzor province in the midst of the oldest wine growing region of Armenia. Rind water supply came from a wonderful spring in the mountains above the village, but the old pipe line was in a state of total collapse. Dr. Yeghiazaryan, as part of his mini-grant with AAA, called it to my attention and said he thought he could fix the problem. Gurgen approached the village with the idea and the village said they would supply the labor if Gurgen would supply the pipe and over-sight for the project. I agreed and assigned Alex, one of our staff, to work with him.

Gurgen and Alex purchased the pipe with MAP funds and a pipe-line more than two miles in length was laid from a small dam built at the spring. Gravity then took the water down the mountain to a holding pond in the village. If you go to the mountain today you may find, written in the wet concrete of the new dam, a notation that says, OK, BRM. We participated in many more water projects during my time in Armenia. On the web, see millerbillr.com.

I appreciated Gurgen's work and supported him on other irrigation projects. I think my judgement was well placed as he is the leader of ANAU (Successor to AAA) in Extension Water Management. His Center is the only Extension Project to survive MAP efforts to integrate Extension into the Armenian program of higher education. Meanwhile, World Bank was successful in creating a Federal Extension Service, typical of World Bank's government to government aid assistance.

More Current Events: U.S. Ambassador Heffern produced a video presentation for YouTube that tells a remarkable story of the **Center for Agribusiness and Rural Development, or CARD,** an institution that MAP created on leaving Armenia. I hope the video is still there. You will find it to be an in-depth presentation of how CARD, under the leadership of Gagik Sardaryan, has continued the work of MAP. You will also see how the work of MAP has been taken over by USAID who began their takeover efforts after a year of observing our results in late 1999.

Heffern's CARD Video on YouTube:

http//www.youtube.com/watch?v=cxwWRNMbc

Other Web-sites that report continuation of MAP efforts:

CARD.Am and ICARE,Am

The **International Center for Agribusiness Research and Education, or ICARE**, reports current work of the Agribusiness Teaching Center, ATC.

Moving Ahead to 2019 and Some Final Results

September 2, 2019---A letter to me from Jeffrey Engels:

"Gagik (Sardaryan) invited me to a Donor Coordination meeting where I met the new Minister of Agriculture Artak Kamalyan (well, actually, since the velvet revolution the Ministry of Agriculture has been dissolved and merged with the Ministry of the Economy) . The meeting was held in CARD's old offices at 74 Teryan Street, above which on the top floor used to be the ATC, although now the entire building is part of the Agrarian University. The Agrarian University Rector is now, of course, Vardan Urutyan, and was great to see him as well. Vardan gave me a tour of the old premises. Attached is a photo of us on the second floor. Also attached is a picture I took for you of your framed letter written in 1999, proudly displayed."

This letter deserves a lot of explanation. To begin, Jeffrey Engels was the last Coordinator of MAP as it ended in 2005. At that time, some of our clientele base were given to USAID who had been coveting the MAP program since the program began to show results in 1999. In year 2000 USAID assigned one of their employees to develop a report on MAP. He came over to see me and was very forthright in asking if I had his permission to interview our staff. Of course, I said yes and he spent about six months researching our project.

The AID employee was so obvious in his work that Ambassador Lemmon even joked about it during what is now an annual wine tasting event that MAP began in the Embassy. Ambassador Lemmon said, "--and USAID may start hosting wine tasting events as they would like to take over the USDA project." Nobody laughed. ----- P.S. Our investment in new Armenian wine production, four new firms by the end of 1999, was one of our first successes in venture capitalism. I still have a bottle of wine produced by the Vyats Dzor winery. Unfortunately, they insisted on naming it VD Wine.

Explanation: Who is Gagik? Gagik Sardaryan is now the head of the Center for Agribusiness and Rural Development (See their website at CARD.am). He was one of my best Armenian Specialists. As I was leaving Armenia in year 2000 I doubled his salary to ensure that all of the projects we started in the past two years would have the correct institutional memory for the next MAP coordinator. I was right. He became the right-hand assistant for every MAP Coordinator until Jeffrey Engels who was the last.

CARD's old offices: CARD inherited MAP office space that I developed during the first few months of my work in Armenia by renovating three unfinished stories of the Armenian Agricultural Academy at 74 Teryan St.

As MAP ended in 2005, MAP still had the office space at 74 Teryan St. and a significant budget. The solution for ending MAP was to continue the work of MAP by creating CARD as a an Armenian NGO to be engaged in service work and in products sold to farmers. In cooperation with the Ministry of Agriculture, CARD opened a series of animal health facilities throughout Armenia. As a profit making firm, they sold farm inputs to production. Perhaps their most recognizable sales items are John Deere tractors and equipment. See more of their work at CARD.am

As CARD was founded using American funds, they needed to name an American founder. Gagik asked me if I would be willing sign as a founder on needed legal documents, I was pleased to oblige. So, in 2005, CARD continued many MAP programs from three floors of office space, about 12,000 square feet of office space for 50 employees, I had developed at 74 Teryan Street using a contract similar to the one I used to build space for the Agribusiness Teaching Center.

Explanation: Who is Vardan Urutyan? Importantly, he is the author of CARE and ICARE. Shortly before I returned to Armenia in 2006, Vardan was hired to replace Dan Dunn as the leader of ATC. Some years later, as the Armenian government began to integrate ATC with ANAU they choose to make Vardan Urutyan the Rector of the new Armenian National Agrarian University and he replaced Rector Terverdian who died several years after our last meeting in 2006. I left Armenia with highest regard for Rector Terverdian. He was dedicated to higher education and loyal to his country. He embraced the concept of an Agribusiness Teaching Center and did more than anyone in Armenia to assure its success.

Velvet Revolution: In April 1918, the corrupt authoritarian government of Armenia was overthrown by a democratic movement without a shot being fired.

Some Endings with Problems:

Although I am pleased to report what I thought was significant progress in economic development of democratic society and competitive market structure, I would be remiss of responsibility if I didn't report some failures. I have mentioned we did have some significant loan failures, but the failure that troubled me the most was my inability to work with the Armenian diaspora.

There are probably more Armenian diaspora throughout the world than there are citizens of Armenia. The most prominent and wealthy are those in California and particularly those around Fresno. No doubt there was disappointment among diaspora in losing the Fresno State contract with AAA, but, in addition, they had a disappointment with their wheat development project in Armenia.

The manager of the diaspora project approached Ambassador Lemmon requesting 700,000 dollars of grant assistance to support their project. They were in fact bankrupt because the Armenian government had raided their offices, taking all of their cash and equipment. Why, that's another story, but you can see it in Armenia Memoir, along with some reasons why Armenians are not always comfortable with their diaspora in America.

As expected, the Ambassador sent them to me. I reviewed their request for assistance and I said could fund the grant of 250,000 dollars they had promised to Armenian farmers. They were growing new wheat varieties thought to improve grain production. Green revolution was expected from their work. I said I could not fund the 450,000 dollars they needed to pay their staff as it would not fit our model of providing venture capital to Armenian firms.

The Armenian manager said he understood and was very grateful for the grant to support their expenses in wheat development. However, the diaspora from California were not so grateful; they were funding the 450,000 dollars needed to pay their staff. A prominent Armenian from California then appeared in my office and told me more than I wanted to hear about what he thought of USDA, and that he intended to take this problem "to the hill".

I told the Ambassador Lemmon what had happened and I said he might get some feedback on the political front. He was visibly upset and somewhat vehemently declared that he didn't give a G— D--- if they take it "to the hill", he was not going to fill their "Iron Rice Bowl." The term "Iron Rice Bowl" is not new; probably he was referring to the concept of a hand-out to the privilidged

The diaspora did take it to the hill; administrators I worked for in Washington thus got a letter from the office of the Secretary of Agriculture. I received more than a letter. I had a Washington visitor from the Secretary's office. There is more in Armenia Memoir. Despite the Ambassador's private response, I am sure that his ability to send the assistance request to me meant that I had taken one for the team.

Ambassador Lemmon was the replacement for Ambassador Tomsen as part of the State Department management of Ambassadors; he proved to be just as much an ally to MAP as Tomsen. So much so that he increased my budget every year I was in Armenia. My budget request for 2001 was 7.5 million dollars, almost double what I started with in 1998. I heard that it was approved.

I made my case for the MAP budget by bringing the Ambassador a steady stream of new food products and success stories to such extent that a member of USAID complained that he(she) was tired of my "Show and Tell" at Country Team meetings. Guilty as charged, I continued to provide a steady stream of results in a different manner. P.S. The only detailed report presented by USAID at a Country Team meeting was a description of how they provided playground equipment for Yerevan schools. Most, if not all of their annual budget of 60 million dollars, was expended on what might be called government to government aid.

The Corruption Problem: Ambassador Lemmon was very much in tune with what he continually described as "widespread corruption". One major irritation was that his staff believed the Armenian government had used 10 million dollars of U.S.

assistance to repay a loan from Russia, but, they didn't say it for public consumption.

I heard early on of common forms of corruption practiced in the former Soviet Union. Several members of the Embassy in Yerevan had served in the newly independent States of the former USSR and said that corruption in States like Moldova and Ukraine were even more susceptible to corruption than Armenia.

The basic concept of corruption, political or commercial, is that if you do something for me I will do something for you without regard to any legal or moral prerogative of the society in which you live. Legal and moral prerogative—what was respected as fair, legal and moral in the former USSR? If you do not understand something of the bankrupt USSR, then you may not appreciate the problem of understanding the meaning of corruption in Armenia and in the other newly independent States of the USSR. So, I attempted to document a few cases.

The basic commerce model is a kick-back scheme. If you buy or sell me something, or provide a favor, I agree that you will receive a kick-back. Just part of business, kickback was an unspoken rule of corrupt commerce. Some residents of Armenia even had a non-verbal way to seal the deal. Tapping somewhere with two fingers, commonly on the side of the face or neck, meant the deal was done; no formality was needed.

Corruption was so normal in the former countries of the former USSR that Ambassador Lemmon said he found it necessary to continually explain corruption. Lemmon was a tennis playing friend of Prime Minister Vasgen Sargsyan and he told the story of how, one day after tennis, the Minister asked in serious tones, "Can you please explain corruption?" Apparently, many of the common business, political, and judicial practices of the USSR were now in doubt by the Prime Minister.

I thought that activities of the local judicial system contributed to failure of loans made my MAP. So I asked a young Armenian lawyer if he could characterize his legal system. He replied that in the former Soviet economy, and continuing today, "possession is more important than ownership". Testimony given to me by many recipients of our non-performing loans indicated they did not feel they were in total possession of their loan funds. Kickbacks and failure of the legal system to prosecute criminal acts, and possibly perpetrated criminal acts, were likely reasons for many of our non-performing loans.

As I reviewed our loan defaults, I believed that many defaults were the result of collusion and fraud. For that reason I kept extensive notes on a case study of our loan to Psank farm.

Psank Farm: On September 2, 1958, a U.S. C-130 was shot down by four MiG-17 and crashed near Psank farm resulting in death of 17 American crew members. A monument was erected near the site, and, during the late summer of 1997, Ambassador Peter Tomsen visited the monument and held a commemorative ceremony in the village of Nerkin Sasnashen.

There, Ambassador Tomsen heard a story of how hail earlier in the year had partially destroyed 35 hectares (about 85 acres) of barley, 100 hectares of corn and 8 hectares of watermelon. The resulting loss was valued at $116,000. The farm would need to sell its inventory of pigs, cows and sheep because they had no feed to take them through the winter. With no milk or meat from the animals, the villagers themselves would be short of food.

Livestock production was a principle activity of the village cooperative farm. Sixty families from four villages including Nerkin Sasnashen, Daftashen, Agarak, and Dprevak had formed the cooperative. The villagers, like a number of village farmers who were given 3 to 4 hectares each via privatization , had chosen to reform themselves into a private cooperative farm, but one that would be managed from the "bottom up", much different from the old days of the Soviet style collective. The new cooperative was Psank farm; the 500 hectares of land owned by the villagers and land leased from local government, allowed them to continue using large farm machinery and familiar techniques to produce supplies of wheat and barley needed for their livestock.

The term cooperative farm is preferred in Armenia where it resembles a western style cooperative. The term "collective " in Armenia, however, carries a connotation referred to by farmers as artificial and undesirable. The term collective, as described by Armenian farmers, referred to a system of privilege under the Soviet system whereby chosen members of the Party colluded to carry out a lucrative profit making business under the heading of a state owned farm, or, a state sponsored collective.

Aid Begins: The Ambassador suggested that as a humanitarian gesture the USDA Marketing Assistance Project should make a loan, or grant, to assist the 60 farmers and 275 inhabitants of the villages. I suggested a $32,000 loan to the cooperative farm, with no collateral, and the village accepted. MAP would have had far fewer headaches had we made a grant. Because: Nothing had really changed the way the people managed their affairs and nothing had changed the environment of old Soviet institutions under which they continued to live during 1998.

Psank farm had problems beyond the loss of livestock and food sources for the winter. These soon surfaced. They were in a dispute with the head of a neighboring village over use of 15 hectares of land leased from local government. Led by the Sasnashen mayor, who was the Psank cooperative farm manager, the villages took their disagreement to the Aratgatsoten Marzpet's (governor of the Marz) office where the Marzpet declared the lease to be illegal.

As an apparent compromise, the regional police chief, not the Marzpet, ordered Psank Farm to turn over the disputed 15 hectares to him for a police farming operation.

Psank farm held a meeting and declared they would not give up 15 hectares to the police chief as they believed they already reached a satisfactory agreement with the neighbor village. The Psank farm manager informed the police chief; who then declared that if the village did not give up the land, the manager would be sorry. A few weeks later he was quite sorry; he was arrested and accused of murdering a gas station owner.

The Psank manager was taken to jail where he was beaten repeatedly in an attempt to make him confess. No confession and no evidence were ever obtained. He was declared innocent by the regional public prosecutor, and released from jail after seven days. His injuries required hospitalization that were apparent to the staff of USDA employees. They reported the manager could hardly walk and could not recognize people more than three meters distant. The manager reported his complaint to Yerevan where Yerevan authorities yielded an answer which said that police were required to use all available means to obtain justice, and the Psank manager should be satisfied that he was cleared of a murder charge.

The beating may have had an even more serious effect. After observing his beaten son, the father of the Psank farm manager suffered an apparent heart attack and died shortly thereafter.

Psank farm reported that the USDA loan allowed livestock feeding operation to go well during the winter and spring. Animals were fed and sold. Prices at Christmas that year were good, and sales were $22,000, which the Psank farm manager took to a local branch of Arm Savings Bank where he received a letter of deposit from the branch manager.

Later in the spring and summer, the farm sold more animals and they were ready to pay back their loan to USDA. Upon visiting the bank to withdraw funds the cooperative farm was told there was no record of a deposit in the bank.

The bank was right, there was no record. What happened to the letter of deposit? The villagers said the bank manager had not deposited the money, but had kept it for his own use. The bank manager was arrested, tried and convicted, and began serving time in jail on his conviction of fraud. Arm Bank, however, refused to accept liability and the money was lost. Can you have saving and investment is this environment?

Bad Luck or Bad Leaders?

Bad weather continued to plague the village. Hail in the following summer again destroyed most of the wheat as verified by Ministry of Agriculture examiners. As fall approached, the animals were again facing starvation. The cooperative farm appealed to USDA MAP to delay payment of the loan so that cash they received from the previous spring and summer sales could be used to feed animals during the winter. USDA accepted the rescheduling of the loan and the farm continued their operations. In the spring, the farm took their herds to high mountain pastures for grazing on new grass in the common grazing area.

Disaster struck from unknown sources. Poisoning by zinc phosphate destroyed most of the herd with a loss valued at $44,000. The family guarding the herd was accused; however, witnesses (?) came forward who said they saw an unmarked police car deliver unknown persons to the area. Suspicion was cast on the regional police, but no evidence was ever found.

The Psank farm manager took livers of several dead animals to a regional veterinary laboratory for examination. He was told the livers showed definite evidence of poisoning and the farm manager should return the next day for a certificate. The Psank manager reported that upon his return the next day the laboratory manager told him that he received a call from the police saying that if a certificate of poisoning was issued, the laboratory manager would be looking for a new job.

The gods of hail had not yet forgotten the village. During the summer following the poisoning, hail devastated the crop for the third successive year, again verified by the Ministry of Agriculture (MOA). Total hail damage for three years, (and a 30-year drought) were estimated by MOA to have generated losses of approximately $300,000.

With few animals and no feed, the cooperative decided to liquidate. They heard the Russian Embassy might be willing to buy their land; they could take the sale proceeds and repay their loan to the Americans. The Russians offered $50,000 for the entire cooperative farm. The village decided to sell and went to the Midland Bank (British owned and now HSBC) to collect certificates of land ownership. The farm had filed ownership certificates as required for registration of their loan from USDA who had used Midland Bank as administrator of strategic loans.

Midland Bank reported there were no certificates on file, although the villagers produced a statement signed by a Midland lawyer who had received the certificates. The lawyer, however, no longer worked for the bank; he had vanished and was never found. A search of his records revealed no certificates. Midland Bank said the land ownership certificates appeared to be irretrievably lost. Who lost them? Are they really lost?

The farm did not sell to the Russians and the Psank manager returned to MAP asking for advice on liquidation. He also indicated in a joking manner that the next step after that would be his hanging, because liquidation would leave the village with no winter resources to buy flour, butter and sugar needed for the 275 inhabitants.

I declared the loan as defaulted and MAP paid the loan amount and accrued interest to Midland Bank; total cost to USDA was $37,000. I offered to continue our village assistance with a grant to the farm.

The Psank farm manager said, however, that a grant would not finally solve his problem because, in addition to his initial loan from MAP, he had borrowed $20,000 additional dollars from persons he could not name (?). The Mafia? Who knows? There are no records.

The Psank farm manager also advised that he did not want a cash grant. He would be appreciative of cash, but it would be a problem. He said emphatically, "please don't give it in cash." Why? A cash grant would be discovered and would attract people who would take it away from them. I was sure he was right and I am reasonably sure it happened to a number of our loans.

As a delivery of commodities might succeed, I offered a humanitarian donation. MAP delivered enough sugar, butter and flour to carry them through the winter.----Although corruption was apparent, I did not give up on the need for venture capital as a loan or a lease.

Assassination of the Prime Minister: The eventual demise of Prime Minister Vazgen Sargsyan illustrates the worst of what can happen in a corrupt State. The Minister, along with Karen Demirchyan, and six Parliamentarians, was assassinated in the Parliament building just one block from our living quarters. Sargsyan and Demirchyan were co-leaders of the Unity Party, a new alliance of Vazgen Sargsyan's Republican Party and former Soviet Armenian leader Karen Demirchian's People's Party. The Communist Party survived the fall of the Soviet Union and did elect members to the Armenian Parliament. Was Sargsyan too close to the old Soviets; or, was this just another political coup?

My sources said that extreme Nationalists (The shooters) opposed the political possibilities of what might happen in Karabakh, an Armenian enclave in Azerbaijan, if the decade-old war between Armenia and Azerbaijan (Muslim) was ended. Many believed that potential concessions to Azerbaijan were a likely cause of the shooting. President Kocharian, a native of Karabakh, assumed leadership of the government following the assassination.

I recall a statement attributed to the mother of the chief assassin. Purportedly, she said, "Someday my son will be seen as a hero of Armenia." From my point of view, I pray that we don't experience a similar level of nationalism in America.

Prospects for peace had looked good. U.S. Deputy Secretary of State Strobe Talbott, a consultant to Prime Minister Sargsyan, was departing Zvartnots International Airport at the time of the assassination. Ambassador Lemmon said he had set aside 10,000 dollars for use when "peace breaks out". It did not. Now, in 2019, the war continues.

-------- P.S. Political murder was common in Armenia during the 1990's. The Armenian "Attorney General" was assassinated a block from my office the week after I arrived in Armenia. Later, Christine and I observed a Russian Lada speed by our house just before a bomb exploded at the nearby home of the new "Armenian Attorney General". However, to my knowledge, MAP loans only faced a threat of violence on one occasion.

My Mistake-I did Business with an Oligarch: The occasion arose because I did not follow my rule of not making a loan to an oligarch of the former communist regime. The reason: There is an important pesticide that was necessary to produce the year's current crop of apples and apricots. As both crops are important in Armenia, I ordered a very large shipment of pesticides from Novartis. We examined the delivery (via Iran, the southern border of Armenia) and found it contained out-of-date chemicals that were totally unusable. Collusion? Imports are not allowed to threaten the market of an oligarch.

The needed pesticide can be produced in Armenia, but I was advised that it used a process copied from a U.S manufacturer. But, faced with losses of the apple and apricot crops, I approved a large loan to a pesticide firm whose owner was a member of the oligarch class of society in Armenia. As his loan went into default he was asked to come in and discuss his plan for repayment. He told our loan manager, Harley Marten, to understand that if anything happened to the oligarch's assistant there would be no witness that a loan had ever existed. The loan was not repaid and perhaps the oligarch's assistant lived to sign-off on another loan

We had loan recipients who complained that they paid "kick-backs" as a form of protection. We believed them and some loans were abandoned because we accepted that loans could not be repaid because of kick-backs. Could we have been deceived? Yes, we probably had some clients who lied; this is one of the risks of using venture capital in economic development.

Using Venture Capital in U.S. Development Policy:

Unpaid loans and corrupt business practices are the major risks in using venture capital in economic development. Yet, without venture capital, the history of America would not include the names of many famous enterprises.

Apple Inc. started as a computer workshop. Genentech was founded by a venture capitalist and the lab-work of a biochemist; these and many like them are examples of venture capital success in the U.S economy. Silicon Valley would probably not exist without venture capital. Most of us understand that America is the richest and most widely developed country in the world because of individual innovation and individual risk takers. Taking a risk on investment in a new firm has been a prime mover in the American economy since the days of pioneers and Conestoga wagons heading west.

Thus, it is not blue-chip companies like Apple Inc. that excite most Americans. Rather, we are excited by small business firms who employ approximately half of our labor force, more than 120 million people, and who create more than 50 percent of all new jobs. Venture capital for small firms is a vital force in the continuing development of the U.S.

Venture Capital Rejected As a Tool of Economic Development?: Ironically, and perhaps sadly, U.S. foreign policy for developing the poorest countries of the world does not embrace concepts of venture capital and personal innovation. Rather, the U.S has embraced humanitarian goals established by 191 members of the United Nations and the 22 largest international development organizations, including the World Bank, the International Monetary Fund (with significant U.S. funding) and our own USAID program that is an important part of the U.S. State Department.

The Millennium Summit of United Nations in 2000 established significant goals of economic development. They were to: achieve universal primary education, promote gender equality, reduce child mortality, improve mental health, combat HIV/AIDS and malaria, ensure environmental sustainability, develop global partnerships for development, and eliminate poverty. Except for the elimination of poverty, all of the goals are easily identified as humanitarian. One cannot argue against the obvious benefits of humanitarian aid, but does it result in economic development?

Who Gets Aid from the Developing Countries: The World Bank model for a Federal Extension Service in Armenia is a prime example of how aid-donors have tried to fund economic development. The world model for development is government to government aid. Venture capital for new firms is seldom mentioned.

For elimination of poverty, which is the obvious goal of economic development, there is virtually no record of supporting new private ventures as part of economic development of aid recipients. Rather, the record for elimination of poverty as a goal of the Millennium Summit shows a major use of development grants going to the central governments of aid recipients. Typical grants have been for government infrastructure projects such as roads, building government financial institutions, providing irrigation canals, providing village wells, hospitals, schools, and building animal health clinics

There has been an overwhelming belief that humanitarian aid and technology transfers from government to government are the keys to economic development. Technology transfer has included subjects such as green revolution in hybrid seed biology and in animal and plant breeding programs. Technology transfer has created a new industry of short-term Washington consultants in the myriad humanitarian aid and technology transfers to central governments. A system of grants to foreign governments and their consultants (and ours) has been the overwhelming way that modern technologies are available to the developing countries. Were there grants to local entrepreneurs? No.

Data on total grants of humanitarian funds to governments of developing countries are difficult to find, but we do know that more than 200 billion dollars have been expended on health issues alone. We know that the budget for the World Bank is annually about 20 billion dollars and recent budgets of our U.S. Agency for International Aid have been higher than 20 billion dollars per year. Data on aid is difficult to find, but my estimates are that humanitarian aid since the end of World War II can be measured in trillions of dollars.

Results of humanitarian aid have been impressive and undisputed, but a billion people still live on less than 2.00 dollars per day. Humanitarian aid has not been enough to solve the long-run problem of poverty. Trickle-down economics has not worked.

Trickle-down economics has certainly has not worked in Honduras and El Salvador. Originally labeled as Banana Republics because they have produced a large percentage of the world market for bananas; little has changed. Principal exports are still from agriculture and citizens abandon their poverty stricken lives for any chance of reaching America. No wall will constrain them. They will find a way until there are good opportunities for staying at home.

The U.S. has made trillions of loans and grants to central governments, some possibly corrupt, in the hope that government projects will produce benefits indirectly for the general population. Noticeably absent have been loans that are a direct benefit to innovative individuals who are beginning new enterprises, even though such innovation has been the source of U.S. success.

Final Observation: In Armenia, loans and leases to new entrepreneurs, new agribusinesses, loans to farmers who support new business and, importantly, investment in institutions, like education to provide local experts, were an acclaimed success in moving toward a market economy and solving the crises of insufficient food supply. But broad based projects targeting use of venture capital are not being repeated. Why? I think there are several lessons and lessons to be learned.

Lessons Learned or To Be Learned

One: Venture capital investments for development that fail in a foreign country are a direct transfer of U.S. tax dollars to people who are not Americans. In some cases, they may not be sympathetic to America. **Two:** Foreign business success in some sectors, like agriculture, will be competitive with U.S. firms. After World War II, USDA was the choice for new aid programs to assist recovery from war-time disruption in Europe. U.S. Secretary of Agriculture Earl Butz turned down the offer because developing agriculture in foreign countries would compete with exports of American farmers; and thus, USAID became the focus of foreign aid. **Three:** The modern model of business is creation of large conglomerates who prefer firms in developing countries to be part of their supply chain. They will not welcome development of local firms who are not under their management control. Not to be forgotten is the control of the market offered by local oligarchs.

What is to be obtained when venture capital succeeds in economic development? The firms created my MAP will evolve just as the Agribusiness Teaching Center evolved and the Armenian Agricultural Academy evolved to be a national University (ANAU). Concepts of market economy, moral and human rights, and entrepreneurial growth learned by ATC students and new entrepreneurs will remain as part of the developing economy, and they will be part of the new institution of Armenian National Agrarian University. Evolution that retains lessons learned for the general welfare of a nation's citizens is the meaning of economic development.

The 65 small agribusiness marketing firms developed by MAP will also evolve Some will become larger, some will fail, some may eventually become part of international supply firms. But,----as they evolve, their efforts will be multiplied in farm food production and in food security. Armenia will become not only sufficient in food supply, but will become exporters of food as, in fact, many of MAP clientele have already done so.

For CARD, the Armenian NGO and successor to MAP, selling John Deere equipment could be the tip of an evolving iceberg. But if the iceberg is part of a real, and competitive market structure, rather than part of a command economy, then, and only then, the evolution of CARD will become part of real economic development. Still to be determined: Will CARD become a competitive firm in a market economy, or, will it remain as an Armenian NGO? In some ways CARD, in its relationship to Armenian government, is like the proverbial bird who flew too close to the sun, but, I remain hopeful for CARD and for competition in Armenia.

Risks of Economic Development without Market Competition

The risk of using venture capital in countries with non-competitive market behavior is real for developing countries and non-competitive behavior is a real risk in America. I have added an addendum to illustrate some of my practical experiences with market competition. I am not naïve about the state of play for competition in America.

Market power and how to use it lies at the core of competitive behavior. Pure and perfect competition will remain as the best theory for maximum social development. But, economic theory still faces significant issues in becoming a "fair" method for market organization and price discovery. I have no illusions about possibilities of non-competitive behavior in small or large firms in the U.S. economy, or in Armenia, but I have no doubt that concepts of "fairness" in market price discovery must become a goal of competitive markets.

A concept of price discovery, rather than price determination, needs to be emphasized. Although the theories of supply and demand to determine price are well known and applicable, fundamentals of supply and demand are constantly changing, resulting in uncertainty and risk. Concepts of fairness in discovery of price are critical for U.S. development.

Our anti-trust laws need to be reviewed for fairness and they must examine use of the internet. Anti-trust concepts and laws were adequate 100 years ago to break-up monopolies like

Standard Oil, but are they adequate to deal with the concept of fairness in modern competition?

Absence of fairness is implied in " **– the ability of a firm, or several firms, to dictate the terms of trade for purchasing, selling or pricing input supplies, products, or services for use.**" Fairness can be defined and fairness must become part of informed regulation.

Concepts of fairness need to be debated and enacted into new anti-trust law to assure citizens that the process of price discovery is fair.   Fairness simply means that citizens believe that prices are "fair". If citizens believe that markets are <u>not fair</u>, democratic principles must allow government to legislate for fair systems of competitive prices and eventual fair ownership of property and services. To be sure, fairness is about what citizens believe; it is a political process. The word "fair" is not part of the lexicon of economic theory, but it cannot be ignored.

Final Comments: The U.S. needs to stop facilitating loans to corrupt, autocratic, and sometimes socialist governments in hopes that trickle-down economics will benefit local people. Trickle down aid is not working for democratic society and market development. At present, our aid programs are alleviating, but not solving humanitarian crises; and they are facilitating command economies.

Market competition, not central command economics, is the only way to discover the set of efficient prices that will maximize human welfare. Concepts of competitive price discovery need to be studied and understood as the basis of fair competition.   Understanding price discovery is difficult, but necessary for fair competition; and only fair competition can reconcile the ever-present conundrum that desires of consumers regarding prices are diametrically opposed to the desires of producers. On the supply side, least cost production remains as a measure of economic efficiency, but if consumers don't have the means and wiliness to pay, products will not sell.

The long-term security of the U.S. depends on continued economic growth in the rest of the world in a manner that follows the American model of success. Warts and all, the model of market economy and democratic society has proven to succeed We need to trust the hope and increased human welfare inherent in finding venture capital for individual firms; firms that will assist market and economic development of poverty stricken countries.

How To Use Venture Capital in 2020: MAP proved that venture capital works in a developing economy. MAP had the necessary and sufficient conditions for success of economic development in agriculture. The necessary conditions are: **1.** Provide technical assistance as education by foreign specialists and develop local educated assistance. **2.** Make venture capital available to local citizens who understand local markets (Now missing in most aid projects): **3.** Finally, the sufficient condition for success is that development efforts must <u>find</u> local entrepreneurs who can actually build economically feasible market infrastructure and supportive institutions.

In developing countries there are three important reasons why there is no appropriate market infrastructure available to farms. One: developing economies have relied on the State to solve the complex problem of efficiently moving farm food production to the consumer table. Two: Developing economies have sought local firms "who fit in" to the supply chains of corporate structures that are national and international in scope. The goals of such supply chains often require extensive investment that does not always match goals of local economies. **Three:** monopoly control of imports was not studied my MAP, but MAP observed significant local monopolies (like pesticides) that were the source of oligarchs detrimental to local market forces.

Whereas, development funding by USAID, and many others, has generally been described as a means of technology transfer, of humanitarian aid, and of loans to questionable governments, MAP went far beyond the traditional model. MAP was successful by using venture capital in creating jobs in new local marketing firms and in solving the Armenian food crisis.

Thus, if you are from USDA and you visit any of the 930 villages of Armenia, you will be met with smiles. You can win hearts and minds, but it is the MAP model, not that of the Army and Peter Van Buren, that will win the day. Van Buren's book is a cautionary tale. Do read it.

Conclusions About Development and Security

American development aid must use venture capital to help undeveloped economies to develop as in the American model. Future security of the U.S. will depend on developing societies that follow the American model of markets and democratic society. No security will result from continuing aid programs that support non-market socialist and authoritarian systems with U.S. aid that is solely humanitarian or military.

Providing venture capital in undeveloped economies will develop world market competitors, but the U.S. will be stronger for it. Adaptation to change is the unparalleled advantage of competition. Withdrawing from the world will not provide the competition a market economy needs for success.

For success, firms that cannot compete must be allowed to fail; failure of firms does not mean a failure of markets, but it does mean a failure to those who think Capitalism is the basis of American society. Capitalism is not a theory and it is not adequate for the task of building a market economy and democratic society; Capitalism is no more than a simple belief system that ownership of capital is a better way to organize society than ownership of capital by government. An economy so organized, and without fair competition, has within it no market forces that can distinguish the difference between profit and greed. But equal opportunity and freedom to compete in open markets will destroy greed.

Market economy understands that capital is only one piece of a puzzle; a puzzle that also includes land (environment) , management and labor. An economy that succeeds must be prepared to pay competitive rents of land, competitive profits to management, competitive interest on capital and competitive wages to labor. Only competition in the markets for basic factors of production will solve what is a developing problem of income distribution.

The absence of competition and the presence of an un-fair price discovery process always suggests that greed can be far more important than profit.

Competitive markets for America's scarce resources are the only way that welfare of consumers and producers will be maximized; although market competition will never be perfect, with appropriate regulation, markets can be thought of as fair.

Unfortunately for competitive markets, many politicians believe that planning a Socialist economy is easier than regulating market competition, ----but Socialism, unlike market economy, has no logical way of allocating scarce resources other than employing gate-keepers of the benefits, and by appeal to humanitarian principles ----and there will never be enough humanitarian dollars to solve economic problems.

The communist variety of Socialism thought that all problems could be "rationalized". If you could plan it, you could do it. History proved them wrong. Socialism shares a fault with Capitalism. Socialism is not an economic theory; it is a simple belief that government is the best way to own and plan a fair use of the nation's resources.

Socialism may provide a minimum social safety net, guarded by the gate-keepers, but it has not shown to produce the growth potential of expanding benefits that Americans have enjoyed from a market economy. The complexity of government and markets is a problem that Socialism cannot solve. Fair market regulation within a democratic process does have a chance for success.

Fair Competition: Although the economic theory of markets studiously avoids use of the term "fair competition", economic theory does show that competitive prices maximize the sum of consumer and producer welfare. Competitive prices result in economic efficiency that is the real driver of a successful American economy. No planned economy can find a set of prices leading to economic efficiency and continued development. The bankrupt Soviet Union proved it by making bread a cheaper feed for pigs than wheat, and with many similar examples of government price fixing.

A word of caution: In America, the incredible waste of food (Perhaps a third of commercial production) going to livestock and fertilizer may be an unfortunate sign of market price failure. Market prices can fail, and certainly markets will fail if not properly regulated.

Practical governance requires refinement and definition of what citizens will accept as concepts of free, but fair, regulation of market power. Because of the high correlation between market power and political power, fair regulation of market power also means political power must also be regulated to preserve democratic process.

Informed regulation is not the enemy of markets and democracy; informed regulation is a force that will enhance markets and democracy. Managers of money, market power and politics must participate in, not resist, the continuing quest for "fair" competition. Fair process can be defined for market power and for political power.

Money, market power and politics, and their high correlation must not be allowed to push the American Presidency into the role of a CEO who "runs the country" and "manages an economic plan for the economy", and does so in isolation from the rest of the world.

There is no historical record of a successful command economy. Too many U.S. citizens are already looking for a President whose plans and commands "can do something for me." But, the purpose of government should be to maintain efficient democracy and market economy so that citizens can do something for themselves and their families.

Venture Capital and U.S. Security

The Marketing Assistance Project (MAP) in Armenia illustrated that economic development did not depend on government plans from a command economy. Development of markets and food security came from people who made innovative use of venture capital when supported by new institutions of education and technical support.

The importance of educational institutions and their work with industry and people may at times seem slow, sometimes halting, in the process of economic development. That slow speed and lack of drama in real development, unless occasional human failing counts, is in sharp contrast to the obvious speed and drama of events that accompany the exploding steel of a cruise missile. But for less than the cost of a cruise missile, MAP provided the only diplomatic effort of the type that will result in a complete victory for U.S. foreign policy. USDA MAP was unusually successful in establishing new educational institutions and markets and farms that have the organic living quality required to last and continue to develop long after the American experts and their dollars have gone home.

Military aid is not discussed in this essay, but it is not forgotten. The history of 8-10 trillion dollars of hard-power military aid in the Middle East dwarfs all commitments to humanitarian and economic aid; and, with 200,000 troops now deployed through the rest of the world, no end is in sight.

The expressed policy goal of our military aid is to assure the security of the United States. That security goal will not be reached unless economic development using the soft-power concepts of venture capital are added to the policy mix.

Amazon Books by Bill R. Miller

Adventures of George and His Friends on Dog Island - Book One   Large Print for Young Readers, 34 pages

Adventures of George and His Friends on Dog Island - Book Two   Large Print for Young Readers, 43 pages

Some History of Statistics and Problems of Measurement For Reader age 9 to 90, No Math Ability Required, 65 pages

Some History of the Second Amendment and the Problem of Guns   Serious Discussion of Historical Precedents for Gun Control, 31 pages

The Millers and Hayes Nature Preserve Some Family History of the Millers of Big Cove, 52 pages

Economic Development of Poland and Armenia 1991-2000   Transition to Market Economy After Communism, 60 pages

Politics, Economics and Religion

    Wide Ranging Analysis of Current Affairs, 36 pages

USDA Marketing Assistance Project—Armenia Memoir

    This is a printed copy of millerbillr.com, 467 pages

Economic Challenges for President Trump

    Economic Outcomes from Political Decisions, 35 pages

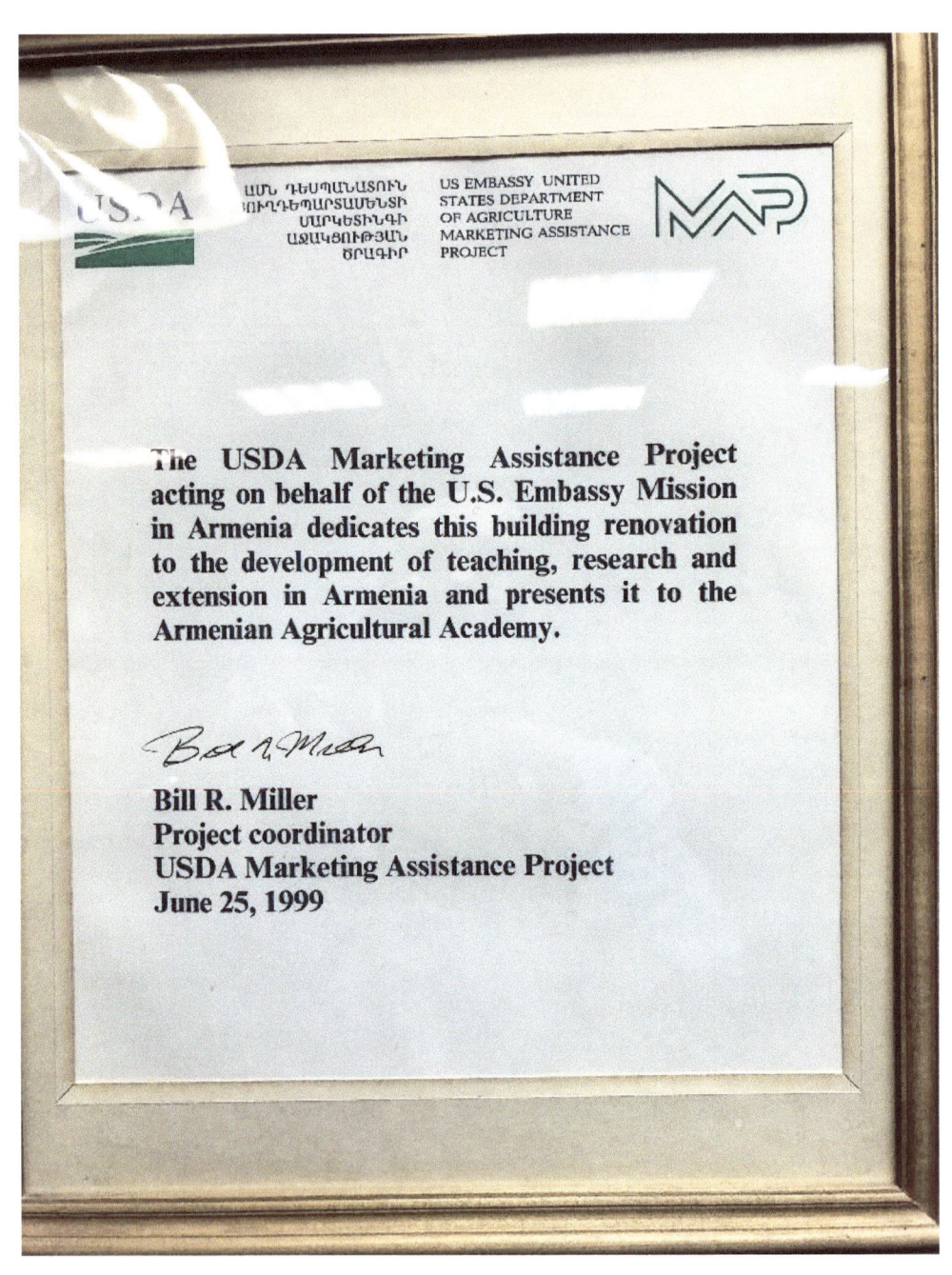

Framed Letter in the Armenian National Agrarian University, 2019

SOME FILE DATA ON USDA PROJECTS IN ARMENIA

While MAP was instrumental in the creation and growth of 65 new marketing firms in Armenia, the total scope of MAP projects supported both agro-processing, individual farmers, Extension projects and higher education were more than 700 and took place in more than 40 projects in each of the nine provinces of Armenia. The final results of MAP initiatives were compiled under direction of the USDA Foreign Agriculture Service (FAS) who renamed MAP as the Caucasus Agriculture Initiative Project. The final results were supplied to me by Karina Grigorian who was my secretary in 1998-2000. She remained with the project until its end in 2005 and she continued after that with the U.S. Embassy.

The total impact of USDA MAP was even larger than reported by USDA-FAS as the United States Agency for International Development (USAID) began support of MAP clients as early as 2001. This alphabet scramble, thus described, represents the kind of "turf battle" for funding commonly seen in U.S. foreign development policy. And, of course, U.S. development policy also provides even more initiatives by supporting loans of the World Bank (WB) and the International Monetary Fund (IMF) in government to government aid.

Total Private Sector Projects Supported in Armenia by USDA, 1991-2005

Projects	Number
Fruit and Vegetable Processing	21
Wineries	10
Milk Collection Centers	17
Cheese and Dairy Products	27
Arid Breeding Center	1
Poultry and Meat Products	16
Production Credit Clubs	50
Village Wells	124
Youth Clubs	127
Agroleasing Equipment	119
Slaughter Houses	6
Applied Research (University)	63
Extension Projects (University)	201
TOTAL	782

* Milk Collection Centers and Cheese and Dairy Products are described collectively in "35 dairy product firms" in other parts of this manuscript. These data also include projects beyond venture funding which were the focus of this manuscript.

** MAP public sector work in the Agribusiness Teaching Center, Armenian Ministries of Agriculture and of Education is not enumerated in the table.

Addendum on Competition

Experience With Non-Competitive Behavior

Market power Definition: Market power is the ability of a firm, or several firms, to dictate the terms of trade for purchasing, selling or pricing input supplies, products, or services for use. And yes,—it does apply to use of the internet for commerce.

Market power is difficult to measure or to even observe. The most obvious evidence is insider testimony or recorded data. This is the only way to definitively prove the existence of market power. In the absence of first-person accounts, the most used description of market power is the four-firm concentration ratio. This ratio has a long history in the study of markets and the ratio describes the percentage by which the four largest firms in an industry control either the sales or purchase of a well-defined commodity or service. Later on, in this essay, I provide some calculations.

Initially, the ratio was accepted as a measure of market power by which a large ratio was associated with a large amount of market power. More recently, apologists for large firms now refute use of the ratio as a measure of market power and allege that it may be no more than a measure showing the degree to which the largest firms are the most efficient.

During my career in Agricultural Economics I attempted to use econometric analysis of observed facts, like the four-firm ratio, as an objective way to describe problems and to offer recommendations for solutions. I believe a review of my publications, more than 100, will show that I achieved, at least, a journeyman status in this effort. Documenting market power was not my major interest, but, along the way I observed that money, power and politics play an important role in creation and control of market power.

Finding enough real data for econometric analysis of market power is rare; and for that reason, simple description and ad hoc reporting of anecdotal one-time events is the only evidence available for revealing market power. For that reason, I am willing to report some of my own anecdotal relationships with market power.

George Wallace and Politics

My first up-close observation of politics and market power came as Assistant Professor at Auburn University and my teacher was Governor George Corley Wallace.

In the summer of 1965 I had finished a year as Assistant Professor of Agricultural Economics. During the year I had worked with Hubert Harris, Professor of Food Science, on several projects. Professor Harris developed the pasteurized refrigerated freestone peach. It was an excellent product, packaged in glass, and not yet surpassed by similar products of clingstone peaches now prevalent in the market.

Professor Harris' work on the product never became a commercial success, despite my efforts to help develop a market. It did lead to my initiative in using his advice to construct a feasibility study of a small size fruit and vegetable processing plant. Professor Harris was perhaps as good in food engineering for small scale food processing as he was in food science.

I won't bore you with what a feasibility study is, but several reviewers thought mine was good. My study caught the attention of several people, including M.L. Glasscock an Extension Economist, who helped me circulate the study among agencies we thought might provide administrative support, or possibly a grant, to build the plant as a demonstration project on the Auburn University campus.

Our goal was to build a model plant to demonstrate efficient food processing and provide new products on a small scale A feasibility study to supply the plans and financial analysis might make it possible. Glasscock thought he knew local entrepreneurs around Alabama who could start such a business. We made one field trip to Bon Secour Bay, near Mobile, where I made a presentation. Glasscock bought a gallon of shucked oysters, but nothing else of any consequence happened at Bon Secour Bay.

Of some consequence, however, was a call from the Governor's office inviting me down to Montgomery for a visit to talk about my feasibility project. I gathered my papers and appeared at the appointed time. George Wallace gave me greetings from behind his desk, reached over to shake hands and asked if I would like to have a coke. Of course, I said yes and he produced two six ounce bottles from somewhere behind his desk. He never mentioned how he heard of my project, but I proceeded to discuss my plans in great detail. I ended my discussion with how I thought it would be great for Auburn University to have such a demonstration project, and how it would be beneficial if new plants could assist development of food processing in local farm communities.

In his best political manner, he says, "Bill I think you are right. We not only need to get this thing built, but we need legislation to provide continuing funds to keep it operational." With that he punched a button on his desk and says, "Would you bring my legislative assistant in here? We've got to write-up a bill and get it into committee."

While the legislative assistant was making his way to the office, George pulled open a drawer and withdrew a 10x10 glossy "Head Shot". With a great flourish of pen, he wrote on the bottom "To Bill Miller from George Wallace." Of course, I said "Thank you very much Governor". The legislative assistant appeared and still in shock and amazement I followed him into an adjoining office where the two of us spent some time outlining some ideas for the bill he would write.

I was jubilant in my apparent success in getting support for the pilot food processing plant, but I was no fan of George Wallace. My meeting with him came after his infamous quote of " - I draw the line in the dust and toss the gauntlet before the feet of tyranny, and I say segregation now, segregation tomorrow, segregation forever", a quote that was the basis for his failed "stand in the school house door" at the University of Alabama. I had no intention of mounting his picture on my office wall, but I did give it to my Mother who thought it quite wonderful. The last time I saw it she had it framed and sitting on a table in her bedroom. My sister says, however, that she never saw the picture. Perhaps my mother was more perceptive of politics than I knew.

The Result: I never heard another word about funding for a pilot food processing plant at Auburn University. A few years later a friend told me that the proposal was never presented in committee. He said when lobbyists for the food industry heard of the proposal they said, "###!! and no *******way is this ever going to happen." He named supporters of large firms. To this day I am reluctant to mention their names. **Lesson learned:** Political power and market power are highly correlated.

George Corley Wallace:

For Wallace it seems that being against segregation was just a means to get elected. When a supporter asked why he started using racist messages, Wallace replied, "You know, I tried to talk about good roads and good schools and all these things that have been part of my career, and nobody listened. Then I began talking about (negroes)*, they stomped the floor"; and "----you know why I lost that governor's race?... I was (out-segged)* by John Patterson. And I'll tell you here and now, I will never be (out-segged)* again."

The Wallace quotes are from Wikipedia: *racial slur N word is omitted. I also substitute the word "-segged" for the N word.

Racism worked for George; following his announced attitude on race he was elected Governor of Alabama for four terms (not all consecutive). Ironically, early in his career he was known as a moderate and was once endorsed by the National Association for the Advancement of Colored People (NAACP). In later life he said the statement he made at the school house door was wrong.

Sam Nunn and Economics of the Peanut Industry

While I was not an admirer of George Wallace, I was a great admirer of Senator Sam Nunn, U.S. Senator from Georgia. The Senator occasionally visited the College of Agriculture on the University of Georgia campus (UGA). I attended every meeting where I was invited and several times I managed to discuss the economics of the peanut industry. He listened I think because he was a land owner near Perry, Georgia and had some peanuts on the farm. He was also Chair of the Senate's Permanent Subcommittee on Investigations and he was a member of the Intelligence and Small Business committees. In particular I discussed some of my concerns for effects of market power arising from concentration of a small number of firms.

At that time, I knew a lot about size and number of firms in the peanut industry. I had a data set that enumerated the disposition from farm to consumer of every peanut produced in the United States. The data came from official sources. If you are knowledgeable of the United States Department of Agriculture you know they have this kind of data for every major crop and livestock produced in the U.S. You may have trouble obtaining it.

My data allowed me to calculate the four-firm concentration ratio for every major sector of the peanut industry. For example, I calculated the four-firm ratio of peanut buying stations by State of location. The ratio ranged from a low of 60 in one State to 100 percent in one important peanut producing State. For peanut butter manufacture in the U.S., the ratio was 53 percent. For peanut shellers, the ratio for the U.S. was 45 percent. For peanut candy in the U.S., the ratio was 66 percent.

For peanut butter crackers, the ratio was 92 percent. Summaries of this data can be found in Special Publication 15 of the University of Georgia College of Agriculture Experiment Stations under the title of "Market Power and Price Discovery".

If you request this publication from the University of Georgia, you will not receive a copy because anti-trust lawyers from New York, Atlanta and New Orleans requested and likely destroyed all available copies shortly after it was published. To my knowledge it was not republished. But, if interested, you may download a draft copy from my site on Researchgate.net where I placed a copy from my personal files.

Senator Nunn said he was interested in my views on market power and he believed it should be looked into. One day while riding an elevator in Conner Hall he said, "Why don't you give me the names of leaders in the peanut industry. Send them to me; I will send subpoenas and we'll have a hearing on the subject." I said I would think about it.

I did nothing else but think about it for about a week. In essence the Senator had given me subpoena power and frankly it scared me. The academics of the problem were a challenge and I believe an important one, but as an untenured Agricultural Economics Professor at UGA did I want to sit down across a table from agribusiness leaders in Georgia and challenge them on a legal basis? Based on my experience with Wallace I believed politics would soon appear.

Who would have been subpoenaed? Some individuals who would have been included were highly regarded graduates and former celebrated employees of the College of Agriculture, University of Georgia. The decision to participate in the proposed hearing meant the possibility of allegations that might seem unwarranted; thus, creating a political fork in the road and I couldn't see the end. To my discredit I was so overwhelmed by the potential politics that I decided not to send names and no hearing was ever held.

Anti-Trust Lawyers and the Peanut Industry: The lawyers who requested, and probably destroyed, all of my copies of publication 15 heard about the publication from me. At the time of publication, I had been hired by the lawyers as a consultant in a case where one of the largest firms in the peanut industry had been accused of violating provisions of the Robinson-Patman Act prohibiting price discrimination. Complainants had a "smoking gun"; someone had been in the room when discriminatory regional prices were agreed on.

I developed an argument for the lawyers that said prices could vary by region because of location advantages that were not necessarily discriminatory. They liked my argument; I liked the lawyers (and I liked my fee) and I got to know them well on a field trip to familiarize them with the peanut industry, but, then the publication came out. The day after requesting all copies of publication 15, they fired me. I never found out what happened in the trial. I heard the trial was held, but the result was sealed. Why?

Price Fixing Observed:

My interest in market development brought me a request to assist in economic analysis of a failed vegetable processing firm. A bankruptcy court had assigned outside managers to "work out a plan to turn the business around" and save as many assets as possible. Responding to the request became an unbelievable opportunity to observe price fixing in action.

I was invited to the first meeting of the bankrupt owners and the new management where the stated goal would be to address opportunities for new ventures. New products were outlined by the new managers and they sounded great to me.

The bankrupt firm was regional in nature as it operated in Alabama and Georgia. They only had one regional competitor, although there were national competitors, and the one regional competitor was invited to the meeting. At the time I remember wondering why you would invite a close competitor to discuss new products, but the reason became clear as the meeting progressed.

The Meeting: The meeting began with lunch in a room which in itself was a page from history. The bankrupt owner was the patriarch of a large family dating to "Old South" times and lunch was served in the patriarch's office; an office large enough to easily seat 10 people, including members of the patriarch's family, the bankruptcy assigned managers, myself and managers of the competing firm.

The lunch table was elaborately set with linen tablecloth, high backed chairs, real silver, bone china and crystal, but before lunch was served a large panel in the back-wall of the room was rolled back revealing a fully stocked bar. A black bar-keeper appeared, white haired, dressed in dark suit with bow tie, and proceeded to take orders. Most of us ordered bourbon and water and lunch was off to a good start.

Following drinks, the patriarch rang a silver bell; two maids appeared, dressed in uniforms, and began serving salads and ice tea, sweet of course. Shortly following were plates of prime rib with trimmings. Desert I don't remember.

We did finally get down to business. I was introduced as someone who would develop an independent cost analysis and feasibility study of new products for presentation to the court. I don't remember all of the discussion regarding the new products, but I do remember the Patriarch (his bankrupt firm located in Alabama) turning to the manager of the competing firm (located in Georgia) and saying "What do you plan to pay for contracts (delivery of raw product) this year? Following a short discussion, they agreed to pay the same price they agreed on last year.

The next discussion took much longer. Discussion centered on counties in Georgia and Alabama where contracts for delivery would be offered. The Georgia firm held the position that they should expand their contract offers in Alabama because the Alabama firm would be cutting back to conserve cash and should concentrate on product development. The Alabama Patriarch reluctantly agreed, with some advising from the court assigned managers, but specified there were certain counties in Georgia where he wanted to preserve his presence.

To my amazement, and within an hour, the farm price for raw product was determined for next year and specific counties in each State were named as the sole contract territory of the designated vegetable processing plant. I have little doubt this was a smoking gun for market power.

What did I do? Sorry to say I did not become a "smoking gun". I decided it would be my word against theirs. At the time I had no tenure; the rule of publish or perish was still in order; I certainly felt the rule would become publish and perish if I published anything I had heard.

Expectations for Competition

Has anything changed? I have my doubts. Elements of market power I have observed are so small in the big picture of agricultural marketing that I refer to my experiences as "country-fried market power". A gourmet serving of market power lies with those giants whose annual sales are measured in billions of dollars and who rank among the largest firms in the world. Agribusiness firms, and other U.S. firms, are becoming larger, more global and their methods more difficult to observe. Undoubtedly, they have market power. Yet, competition must have informed regulation and enforcement of law if competitive markets are to survive. Do voters have the political will to make it so? I continue to believe they do once the problem is adequately described.

My anecdotal comments about markets are raw and may indicate that I am pessimistic about the future of America. I am not. Though threatened, the spirits of reformation and revolution that led to democratic freedoms and the rise of a market economy are very much alive. But, whenever these ideas have been defeated, as history shows they can be, succeeding central command economies and Kingdoms eventually become bankrupt for failing to provide what they promise their citizens.

Bankruptcy of a command economy does not come easy or quick. Witness the slowly crumbling Soviet economy as it took place over about 80 years. No, it was neither the Pope, Ronald Reagan nor Gorbachev that brought down the former Soviet Union. Corrupt business practices and despotic leadership in a command economy resulted in inability to discover competitive prices followed by economic inefficiency and bankruptcy on a monumental scale.

Not long after the U.S. Constitution was ratified in 1788, the dangers of failed society in the United States were clearly recognized by Alexander Hamilton. In 1792, Hamilton saw possible failure as storm and whirlwind led by a despotic commander.

Hamilton wrote: "Those then, who resist a confirmation of public order, are the true Artificers of monarchy—not that this is the intention of the be suspected. When a man unprincipled in private life desperate in his fortune, bold in his temper, possessed of considerable talents, having the advantage of military habits—despotic in his ordinary demeanour—known to have scoffed in private at the principles of liberty—when such a man is seen to mount the hobby horse of popularity—to join in the cry of danger to liberty—to take every opportunity of embarrassing the General Government & bringing it under suspicion—to flatter and fall in with all the non-sense of the zealots of the day—It may justly be suspected that his object is to throw things into confusion that he may "ride the storm and direct the whirlwind."

(From Alexander Hamilton—Enclosure: Objections and Answers Respecting the Administration, 18, August 1792)

I believe Hamilton would agree with me if I could explain to him that fair competition results in public order, desperation in fortune leads to greed and market power, scoffing at free competition is to scoff at the principle of liberty and that bringing government under suspicion is one of the worst ways to resist market and political regulation.

Concerned citizens should be aware. The absence of free democratic society and a competitive market economy will attract despots who claim that a great leader is needed to control the storm and whirlwind generated by unregulated greed.

www.ingramcontent.com/pod-product-compliance
Lightning Source LLC
Chambersburg PA
CBHW051158220526
45473CB00003B/816